KARA
and the
MAGIC CAMPER

Written by

Jessica Policarpo

Illustrated by Yvetta Douarin

First published in 2024

Written by Jessica Policarpo
Illustrated by Yvetta Douarin
Book design by Bryony van der Merwe

ISBN: 979-12-210-6727-9 (hardcover)
ISBN: 979-12-210-6728-6 (paperback)

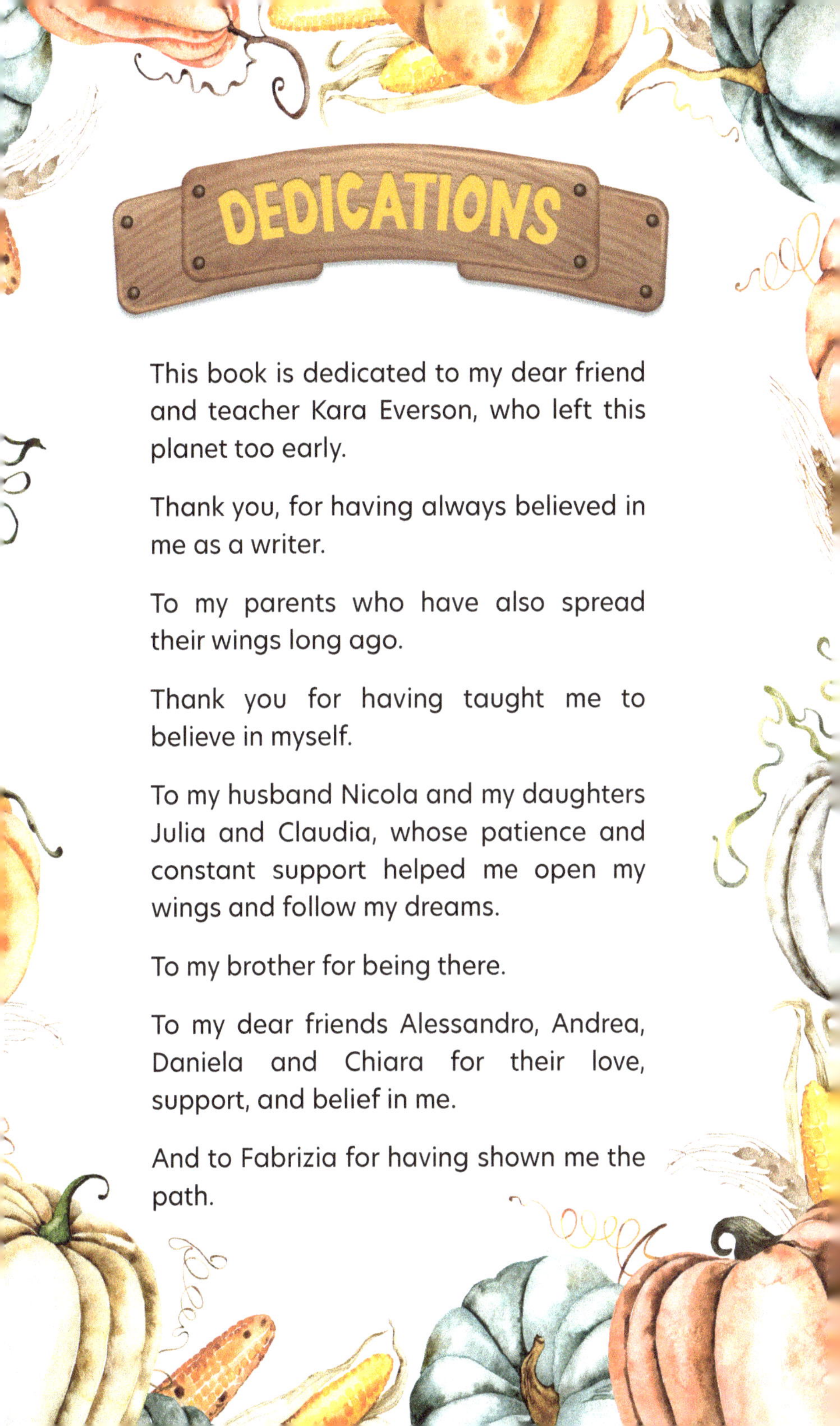

DEDICATIONS

This book is dedicated to my dear friend and teacher Kara Everson, who left this planet too early.

Thank you, for having always believed in me as a writer.

To my parents who have also spread their wings long ago.

Thank you for having taught me to believe in myself.

To my husband Nicola and my daughters Julia and Claudia, whose patience and constant support helped me open my wings and follow my dreams.

To my brother for being there.

To my dear friends Alessandro, Andrea, Daniela and Chiara for their love, support, and belief in me.

And to Fabrizia for having shown me the path.

CONTENTS

Let's meet the Characters 7

Chapter 1: A typical week day
on the farm 20

Chapter 2: On the weekend 28

Chapter 3: The plan 62

Chapter 4: The field trip 94

Chapter 5: The magic camper 108

Chapter 6: Back home............................. 146

Let's
meet the
Characters

Kara

Kara is a 12-year-old girl. She lives on a farm. Her parents are away for a while with her baby brother Richard, and she takes care of the house with Grandma Violet (who mostly sleeps on her rocking chair on the porch at the back of the house.) She doesn't mind them being away—well, let's say she's used to it. They travel a lot for work and take Richard with them because he's too small to stay at home. She's never really alone because all of her friends live there too and they take care of each other and she likes doing her own "thing." Deep inside, though, she is jealous of her brother being away all the time with her parents, seeing beautiful and different places. She never spends much time with them and she's always wanted to travel. For now she does that in her dreams, and often fantasizes out loud in front of her cat Pebbles. No one else knows about her secret dream.

She loves making herb teas and takes care of her lovely vegetable garden. Her mother taught her how to recognize different herbs and how they are used for different things. Kara is a "happy go lucky girl" but when she gets angry, she gets really angry. She doesn't like it when people disrespect her and make fun of others. There is one special thing about Kara that makes her different from all the other girls of her age: apart from the fact that she always thinks of others first and puts their needs before hers, she also lives in the same house as her farm animals and they are her best friends...

The Professor

The Professor (that's what they call him, nobody knows what his real name is) walks like humans do, on two legs. He can be serious even with bunny ears on his feet. The Professor has a sweet sense of humour. When he laughs, he snorts, so he doesn't do it often but he smiles a lot with his eyes. I must say he is quite a messy type of guy. He's the silent type. Everybody considers him to be the wise one; he reads a lot and has books everywhere. He and his best friend Slumber, the dog, often discuss technical things needing to be fixed around the house as well as any other type of topic. They are the type of people you would call best friends. He dreams of having a big library.

Tobia the mole

Tobia is quite a particular type of mole. He hates wearing glasses so he uses contact lenses. He goes around with a pair of trunks and wears boxers at night. He's a perky fellow and gets offended very easily. He's got a bit of tummy problems too and often farts. That's why he goes around with perfume in his pocket. His recent plan is to build a fence around his hole but he's unsure because that would give up his "identity" as a secret agent, the informer of the farm.

The Hens: Elsa, Eve, and Gladys

Elsa is a very domestic hen. She's the farm's cook and "mother" to them all. She cooks all day and loves tasting the food she makes. She's working on her cookbook, a collection of all the favourite recipes of the house members. Elsa lays her eggs in silence in the morning and then gets up to do the things she loves.

Eve is a painter. She's slightly snappy and loves to poke into other people's business (it's a sister thing). She doesn't do much apart from paint and look out of the window with her binoculars. Sometimes, she helps her sister Elsa in the kitchen.

Gladys loves opera and sings when she lays eggs or showers. She likes to design clothes but hasn't had her designs turned into clothing yet.

Slumber: The dog

Every farm has a dog and so does this one. Slumber likes to joke and loves the family. He aims to protect them all. He's especially fond of Kara whom he's known since the first day he got to the farm when he was just a puppy and so was she. Slumber is always doing something: he's the electrician, the bricklayer, the mechanic and whatever technical issue there is to resolve, he goes to the Professor. He's the farm fixer.

So that is it. These are all of Kara's friends. They are quite a team and they love each other very much. They love life on the farm and spending time together.

The Farm

The farm is a typical New England barn, with a lovely big brown roof and stone walls. A huge red barn door opens up to the living room (which used to be the milk room) with a huge red carpet in the centre of the room. Directly opposite the barn door is a very big fireplace. On top of its lovely mantelpiece are the family portraits. Two sofas are arranged around the fireplace, burgundy blankets hanging over the sides. Armchairs sit on either side of the fireplace, with a card table in front of one sofa and four big soft pillows scattered on the carpet.

The kitchen is right next to it. It contains a very big table, a chair on each end, and benches on the sides. On one wall in front of the dinner table, there is a very big cooker with two sinks. Yellow polka dot curtains hide shelves under the sink. Shelves on top of the cooker are filled with books.

The hens live under the roof, upstairs, each with her own bedroom and a nice living room overlooking the farm. Their "hut" has large windows with beautiful flowers hanging off of them.

There is a round table with three chairs around it, a lovely yellow tablecloth, a big glass vase with fresh flowers, beautifully arranged, on top of it. The light from the window lightens up the whole room. They also have three large comfortable sofa seats where each sister lays her eggs and chatters away. They use binoculars for spying and keep a big notebook to track everything that happens on the farm. In case of problems, they all have everything written down as evidence. They don't have a kitchen but a small stove with a food storage cabinet.

Kara lives on the same floor. Her room is huge, with a big double bed and lots of colourful pillows. She has a small toilet inside her bedroom with a shower and a small stove to cook herself something if she wants to. Her parents' room is farther down the hallway and there is a small baby room for Richard.

The Professor lives outside in a shed next to the vegetable garden. His room is small. He has a tiny kitchen with a round table and chairs. He has a small bed (even though he is quite tall, his bed is tiny and he loves to sleep with his feet on top of the bed frame); a sofa (same story as the bed); a very old rocking chair; and a fireplace, which is almost always on. He reads on his rocking chair and never eats at the table but places the plate on his legs. His coffee table has a collection of tea cups on it which he leaves and forgets. (Well, he doesn't really forget them, he just ignores them and pretends he can't see them). The Professor's bed is always unmade. He often sleeps on the rocking chair and leaves the door slightly open. At the back, there is a small house with a porch where Granny Violet lives.

On the other side, a little closer to the farmhouse, is Tobia's den. He lives in a hole just outside the farmhouse. There's a bed, a red carpet, a red hammock, a stove, and a little table with two wooden chairs. He also has a periscope glass which he uses to spy on everyone, especially Gladys. He has a small shower; he loves taking showers. As soon as he walks in his home, he changes into his night wear, his slippers, and his super big glasses. His lenses irritate his eyes but he won't admit it.

The whole farm is surrounded by a fence and next to the entrance gate is Slumber's little guard dog house. He lives next to the gate and guards the house. His hut is quite a simple one with a bed on the floor, a simple blanket, a small brown carpet, a single armchair with a foot rest, and a tiny bedside table. His kitchen consists of a cooking stove, a shelf, a table and two chairs, an old garden rake to hang his clothes on.

A typical week day on the farm

Actually, there is no real typical day on the farm. As life teaches us, every day is different and we must always expect the unexpected. So let's say that this was more of a daily routine.

The day usually began with the hens waking before anyone else. They would get dressed, wash up, make some warm tea, and scramble up on their armchairs to lay their fresh eggs whilst chatting away loudly (as chickens do) about the farm news...even if there wasn't any because the day hadn't started yet but let's just say that chatting was what they did best no matter what it was about!

Elsa would go downstairs and start putting on the porridge and tea for the whole family. The next to wake up was usually Kara. She would wash her face, get dressed, and go down for breakfast. Then she would go back up to brush her teeth, make her bed, and catch the bus for school.

Slumber, faithful as ever, would walk her to the bus stop, which was just outside the farm gate. Then he would slowly start going towards the farm to have breakfast with his friends.

Firstly, he would drop by Tobia's to make sure he was ok (without making it obvious, he knew Tobia was prickly). He would drop by and say good morning to the Professor (who usually was still sleeping) and finally he would go to have a nice cup of tea with the hens. (All three of them would be downstairs and around the table at this point).

Tobia, on the other hand, would wake up after a while (he loved sleeping in) and slowly, very very slowly, he would go to the bathroom, wash his face, put on his slacks and his contact lenses, and go to his periscope to see what new adventures his surroundings would bring him. After having made sure that everything was in place, he would slowly get out of his hole and go and have a cup of tea with the hens. Every morning Elsa, Eve, Gladys, Slumber, and Tobia would have breakfast and porridge all together, laughing and cackling away, as friends do. Then each one would go back to doing his own things. Elsa would then go and wake the Professor.

The Professor would go to the bathroom and sit right back down on his rocking chair, sip his tea whilst looking outside, and eat his porridge. He was never in a hurry. Usually, Slumber would drop by around that time of day.

That's what they loved about their life. The simple routine meant they knew exactly what was going to happen next, or almost.

Slumber would go and fix something around the farm.

Tobia would go around to see what was going on, looking around to see if he could find some new adventures. (Actually, he was the only one that would go and check on Grandma Violet).

No one really noticed Grandma because she was such a silent type. She was very old and very proud of her little granddaughter. She wouldn't say much, she often laughed when she heard Kara speak to all her animals. She couldn't hear them talk. They were just farm animals to her.

The hens wouldn't usually stay in the kitchen after breakfast, except for Elsa who would clean everything up and start getting something ready for lunch and dinner. Gladys would usually go up to her room, choose her outfit, get everything ready and think of what would inspire her day.

Eve on the other hand was very quick. She would go up to her room, get changed, and go down the stairs as fast as she could to pick flowers. Usually around one o'clock, the bus would stop in front of the fence. Slumber, punctual as ever, would open the gate for Kara.

Kara usually dropped by to give Grandma Violet a kiss. Then she'd run up to her room, take her clothes off, put something comfortable on and jump on the bed. She jumped on the bed right after school, she loved to feel how soft the mattress was and she usually dozed off letting all the stress of the day disappear.

The smell of the farm would always bring that happiness back into her, especially this smell of Elsa's lovely sauce. The Professor was always the last one to arrive, and just before him Tobia, obviously complaining about something. As long as there was something to complain about, he was happy. The flavour of Elsa's food was so delicious, no one spoke. After lunch everybody would help out with the cleaning up, except for the Professor, of course, he would just doze off on the rocking chair and Slumber on the couch right next to him. Kara would do her homework and Elsa often sat right next to her to help. After that, Kara would go around the farm to collect the eggs and the flowers and herbs and check that everything was prim and proper.

Late afternoon, she would often go and sit with her grandmother and watch her sleep. At dinner, they all would all meet again. In winter, Elsa made soups, whilst in summer, they ate lots and lots of salad and fresh vegetables from their vegetable garden. They didn't eat meat (it was just so disrespectful to eat meat on the farm). Mostly, they ate potatoes, carrots, tomatoes, lettuce, fennel, cabbage, and eggs. They loved eggs and beans, lots of beans. After dinner, they all stayed and chatted. Some read a book while others watched the fire. The Professor, Slumber, and Tobia would usually play a game of cards or two, all sipping on their herb tea.

After a while, they would go up to their own beds.

"Goodnight, everyone, *see you tomorrow.*"

(*See you tomorrow* was a sentence they would always say, it gave them a sense of comfort and security.)

"Goodnight, Kara, *see you tomorrow*, sleep tight."

That was the end of a "typical day" at the farm.... the typical daily routine of our animal friends and Kara.

On the weekend

It was Saturday morning. The clouds in the sky and the fresh air were the first signs that autumn was on its way. Everyone was sleeping and the farm had a sort of magical silence about it. All except for two...Tobia and Slumber.

Slumber was always an early bird. It was just in his nature to get up early. As soon as his nose smelt the day, his eyes would open. He made himself a fresh cup of coffee, put on his slacks and shoes, and sat outside on his rocking chair facing the farm. His house was a sort of "Check out Point." He just loved to take care of everyone and protect them, it was his job, it was just what being a dog was about.

That's what made him who he was. As he rocked, he noticed some movement around Tobia's house so he took his binoculars and there it was, Tobia was sneaking out of his tunnel.

"Sneaky fella, what on earth is he up to this morning?" Slumber asked himself. Tobia had his detective clothes on with dark glasses. His coat was too long so he kept tripping on it, which made Slumber giggle.

At a certain point, he disappeared behind the pile of earth which was actually the top of his house. Slumber slowly and carefully moved around so he could see him better. By the time he got around, Tobia had disappeared. Slumber moved silently closer to his tunnel to take a better look ... he could just faintly make out a small black figure running into the woods...

Well, I'll be... thought Slumber. *I must go and report this to the Professor.* And off he went.

It was very early and the Professor was sound asleep on his little bed with his feet sticking out at the end of it. It was quite a funny sight to see such a big goat on a small bed, but now was not the moment for that funny thought. Slumber sneaked into the house and closed the door behind him.

"Professor, wake up, wake up, it's quite important that you wake up," he said in a slightly louder voice…

"Who's that! What did you say? You trespasser! What do you want?" He scrambled up, quite confused and upset.

"It's only me, old chap, it's Slumber."

"Slumber, what on earth are you doing here? What time is it? What is going on!?"

"Everything is fine, I just need to talk to you."

"Well, if everything was fine, you wouldn't be here now, would you? Where are my slippers, what is going on?"

"Here they are. I'll make you some tea and then we can talk."

"You most certainly will, it's the least you can do after this scabble of a wake up you put me through."

When the Professor finally calmed down and had a sip of tea, Slumber told him all about what he had seen.

"Well, well, well, this is quite something to wake me up for. What is that lad up to now!"

"I thought you might say that. I'm glad you did actually. I have no idea, but we must find out."

"Yes, we absolutely must, now give me some more tea, if you would, please, and let's talk about this seriously."

In the meantime, Tobia had come back, rushed into his tunnel home,. his feet were all muddy so he jumped into the shower, dried, put his clothes and perfume on, and walked over to the farmhouse for Saturday morning breakfast.

"Good morning Tobia," said Gladys.

"Good morning, Gladys, you look lovelier than ever this morning."

"Oh, don't be silly, you'll make me blush," she said with a smile as Tobia winked at her.

"What's for breakfast? Good morning, ladies, Tobia," said Slumber as he walked into the farmhouse.

"Good morning, everyone," said the Professor.

"Well, you're up early this morning, Professor," said the hens almost all together.

"Yes, well, I fell out of bed and here I am."

"Tobia, good morning, old chap, what are you up to this morning?"

"Up to? Nothing, why? I'm reading the paper as always, why would I be up to something?"

"No reason, it's just a saying, don't get so nervous."

"I'm not nervous."

"Well, that's enough now, I've made pancakes, come to the table all of you and let's have breakfast."

"Wow, pancakes, how come?" said Slumber.

"Are you complaining?" Tobia asked.

"No, I'm not complaining, I'm just surprised. You seem a bit tense this morning."

"I'm not tense."

"Will you both just stop that and eat?"

"Well," said Elsa, clearing her voice. "I wanted to try something different and since I don't have a lot of variety in the breakfast chapter, I thought about pancakes. I'm sure Kara will like them."

"I'm sure we all will," said the Professor.

"I'm glad you've started on your book again," he said with a smile. "Anything else new this morning?"

"Nope, nothing, why? Why should anything be new?" said Tobia.

"Stooooooop thaaaat," sang Gladys in a loud screeching pitch....

Nobody dared to speak after that... except for Kara who walked down in her pyjamas. "What's going on?" she asked in a sleepy voice.

"Oh, dear, we've woken you up. Nothing is wrong, dear, I'm so sorry, you were sleeping so well. Come and sit down and have a cup of tea and pancakes."

They all sat down to finish their breakfast with their heads down in silence while Slumber and the Professor looked at each other knowingly.

"Lovely breakfast, Elsa, thank you, you should make them every Saturday," Kara said as she dragged her feet to the sofa, pulled up a blanket, and fell asleep again.

"Aha!" said Tobia while turning the pages of the newspaper.

"What's that about?" said the Professor.

"Nothing, I just hit my toe."

The Professor looked under the table and saw Tobia's feet comfortably crossed on the seat cushion.

"What you looking at?"

"Oh, nothing, I thought I dropped something."

Slumber had sneaked outside the farm gate. He followed Tobia's footprints until he got to the beginning of the woods.

"Well, I'm certainly not going in there on my own. I must call the Professor and go with him." He headed back to his house.

In the meantime, the Professor had managed to make his way out of the house with the newspaper while nobody was watching. Tobia had gone for a walk with Gladys to collect some vegetables for lunch, or that's what they had said at least.

The Professor walked slowly to Slumber's house and knocked at the door three times. "Tap tap tap." He let himself in.

"Why do you knock if you come in without me asking who it is?"

"Oh, don't be so formal." The Professor couldn't exactly fit in the little house and was crouched with his head curved down. "You really should think about getting something bigger and more comfortable."

"It's just fine. Sit down, I've made some fresh tea."

"Oh good, it's about time."

Slumber stared at him in awe. "Got the paper?"

"Yes, I have, dear fella."

"Well, what are you waiting for?"

"Tea, of course."

"Oh, stop that, the kettle is on the stove. Open the paper. Let's see what that was all about."

The two of them turned the pages and looked at all the articles but they couldn't find anything suspicious. They were now on their third cup of tea; frustration was starting to fill the room.

"We must be missing out on something."

"Obviously, Slumber, that is quite obvious, but WHAT! That's enough. I must take this back home and read it comfortably. I can't work in this tiny home with no tea left."

"Please yourself, Professor, but I don't quite appreciate the tone you are using, and may I remind you that we have been drinking tea for the past few hours!"

"Tone! Tea! What ARE you blabbing about? This is serious business and you've just not taking it seriously enough!"

"Ha! Would you like to talk serious? Well then, get ready for tonight. We will meet here at 7 p.m. and go into the woods."

"The woods!! Are you quite mad!? I'm not in any condition to go into the woods," replied the Professor.

"Well, I can't go alone, and it seems you're the one that it not quite serious about this."

"Well, after this, I think I shall go to where life treats me better." And off he went, the newspaper well hidden inside his overcoat.

A lovely smell of sauce filled the air and, as if by magic, everyone was suddenly gathered around the lunch table. There it was right in the middle of the table, spaghetti, the Saturday lunch favourite.

The air was chilly and there was a slight wind sweeping up the leaves. It was 7:00 p.m. on the dot and the sun had started to leave space for the evening moon. Slumber wore his high neck sweater and coat and was sitting on his porch seat staring impatiently at the house. Finally he saw a shadow appear. It was the Professor with a long overcoat and an elegant scarf, puffing away on his pipe. The two said nothing. They made no eye contact and started to head towards the woods at a proper distance for two who had quarrelled. But as they got closer to the dark trees, the distance became less and less until they found themselves almost shoulder to shoulder. The wind had lifted and dark surrounded the two friends as they slowly entered the trees.

The trees were so tall and they looked down as if they were watching and listening in a very overpowering manner. The two animals could feel the power that surrounded them and they felt quite small and lost. They still were not speaking. Neither of them wanted to speak first so they casually walked deeper and deeper into the woods with no point of reference or plan. Suddenly their feet started feeling wet and their shoes were heavy and stuck.

"Oh."

"Hmm."

"Yes, well, hmm, maybe you should look where you put your feet," whispered the Professor.

"Oh, I should, should I, and you were looking, were you?"

"What has that got to do with it? It was your idea in the first place, you're the one that got us stuck in this."

They suddenly shut up as they saw a tiny light in the middle of a big muddy lake smack in the middle of the forest.

Their eyes widened and they didn't know whether to laugh or just stare for the sight of what they saw was both funny and quite strange

Right in front of them was a camper, big and white and stuck in the mud. The light was on and there he was, Tobia, dancing on the table and doing the moonwalk to some very loud music. He had nothing on except boxers, a scarf, and dark sunglasses.

"Oh, my goodness," the friends uttered at the same time.

"Now that's a sight I never thought I'd see in this lifetime," said Slumber.

"Well said, old chap, who would have thought? Never in a thousand years could I ever have imagined something like this!"

They laughed and hugged each other. They couldn't keep their balance for their shoes had sunk in so deep, they were literally stuck in the mud!

The light suddenly went off and silence surrounded them once again. The trees swooped in the wind and the leaves rustled. It was as if the forest had gained its power again and was laughing at the sight of it all. Nothing felt funny to them though and they all three (including Tobia) froze in fear. The door of the camper opened and out came Tobia, all dressed up for winter with a small torch which he held in his shaky hand...

"Who's there?" he said with a string of voice...wishing he had never done this. He stepped on the plank of wood he had set outside the door to cross from the camper to the grass and walk over the muddy lake...

Nobody moved except for the branches. The two trespassers just stood there frozen, holding each other...their eyeballs popping out of their heads as the light of the torch shone in their faces.

"What on EARTH are the two of you doing here!" Tobia yelled angrily.

The Professor cleared his voice. "Looking for mushrooms?" he said with a silly smile.

They all three laughed, they laughed so hard their tummies hurt. The Professor and Slumber started losing their balance and held onto each other even tighter to avoid falling into the mud. At the sight of that, Tobia laughed even harder! They all froze when they heard a branch breaking in the wind and landing not too far from them.

Tobia took a rope and tied it around a tree. After he had thrown it to them, they started pulling on it to get out of the brown mess they had gotten themselves into. The Professor's shoe got stuck and his foot slid right out of it as he pulled himself out.

"Nooo," he shouted, but it was too late now. Fear had gotten into them and they ran away, in a frenetic sort of crazy run, out of the woods and right back to the road that let them back to the farm. No one had any idea how they found their way out of there. They sat on the floor, panting and giggling...

"Right, we'll meet back at my place, I need a cup of tea and a house where my head won't hit the ceiling."

Slumber was about to comment but he held his breath. "Righty oh Professor... off we go."

It was almost midnight and the three of them sat around the table in their underwear with a warm cup of tea in their hands. It was quite a sight...

"Well, spit it out, Tobia," said Slumber.

Tobia spat out a leaf he had probably gobbled up in the rush to escape.

They all cracked up.

"That's not exactly what I had in mind," said Slumber, still laughing.

It had been quite an adventure and I must say one of the best nights they had had in a long time! The two guests scrambled off, each in his own direction so as not to look suspicious. Slumber went inside his house, took his wet clothes off, and jumped into bed. They still didn't know what Tobia had been doing in that camper *but we'll deal with that tomorrow*, thought Slumber as his eyes closed and he drifted off into a deep sleep. Tobia, on the other hand, came home to find his doormat had been moved. He looked under and found a note from Gladys.

WHERE ON EARTH ARE YOU? GLADYS.

Oh dear, thought Tobia. *That's not what I need right now.*

He slipped into his house, looking around suspiciously, and jumped into bed with no clothes on. He was quite tired. *It must be all the dancing*, he thought, giggling himself to sleep.

There was someone who wasn't getting any sleep but was silently watching from her telescope behind the curtain while the whole farm lay snoring away.

Sunday morning was usually quite a lazy morning for them all. Each animal—and Kara—would walk into the farm and make themselves something for breakfast and just "hang around the house." There was a lovely carrot cake, which Elsa had made, on the kitchen table; that wouldn't last long.

Gladys was sitting on the armchair next to the fire with a glass of cocoa, wrapped in a small blanket and dozing away. She was quite tired. Who knows how long she had stayed there staring at the telescope hoping something suspicious would come up? I think she might have even fallen asleep in the meantime. At around 6:00 a.m., there was quite a crash and a cackle and then down she came to make herself a cup of something warm. She hadn't even been able to lay some eggs, her mind was so preoccupied with her thoughts.

Tobia walked into the room on his tiptoes. "I can hear every step," said Gladys, looking at him with a hard gaze.

"I can explain everything," he said in a shaky tone.

"Of course, and you WILL," she replied.

Tobia made himself a VERY strong cup of coffee and just as he was about to open his mouth to speak to Gladys, down came the two sisters.

"Well, bad timing as always," Gladys snapped at them.

"Good morning to you too, sister love," they said together.

She looked away; this just wasn't a good start to the day.

As the sisters sat cackling away around the table, eating cake and drinking tea, in came The Professor and right behind him, Slumber.

"Good morning, ladies, Tobia," said the Professor.

"Good morning, Professor," the ladies replied.

"What in heaven's name have you got on your feet??" asked Elsa, giggling.

"On my feet?" he replied as he looked down. "Oh dear." He ran out, embarrassed, back to his house.

"Slumber," he whispered as he dashed off.

"Professor," replied Slumber with a smirk on his face as he caught a glance of his pink rabbit slippers.

Nobody knows I wear these slippers except for my faithful friend Slumber, thought the Professor as he quickly changed into his shoes. He had to put another new pair on because he only had one shoe left from his old pair. The other one was stuck in the mud in the woods! He hurried back. "Now what am I supposed to say?" Panic shone in his eyes as he returned to the farm.

Nobody asked anything so he sat on the rocking chair in front of Gladys frozen, like a stockfish.

"Here you go, old lad," said Slumber as he passed him a warm cup of tea and a slice of cake.

"Thank you, Slumber."

So, there they were, all four of them sitting one in front of the other in utter embarrassment and silence just staring at each other.

Tobia moved his eyes to the Professor, pointing them towards Gladys, and the Professor stared at him, trying to understand. Slumber caught that stare and turned around to look at Tobia as he made the same move with his eyes. Slumber motioned to Gladys with a slight tilt of his head to the Professor who suddenly said, "Oh, no."

"Oh YES," said Gladys looking at all three of them. "Yes indeed."

They all three put their heads down and stared at the insides of their cups, uneasy and with no clue how to proceed.

"Good morning, friends," said Kara with a cheery voice as she walked in with a basket full of apples and carrots from the garden.

"Grandma Violet loved the carrot cake, Elsa, and so did I, may I have another slice please?" she asked as she sat down next to Slumber.

As she sat there eating, she looked at each one of them and noticed something was not quite right.

"Ok, spit it out," she said.

To the sound of those words, the three males laughing so hard, they almost choked on their tea!

"Ok, that is ENOUGH," screeched Gladys in a loud chicken voice.

"Enough of what?" Elsa asked. "You've woken up in quite a mood for a Sunday morning, haven't you, sister dear?"

"Don't you sister dear me," she replied.

"We've got quite a puzzle to put into place, haven't we, gentlemen?"

They stared at the inside of their mugs again. None of them knew what to say or do, so they just sat in silence.

The next few hours were quite an inquisition for the three gentlemen as they were suddenly surrounded by the ladies and Kara with their arms crossed, staring at them and filling the room up with questions.

"What puzzle?"

"What have you been up to?"

"Where were you last night at 8:00 p.m.? And why did you return to your house at midnight?"

"Midnight?" said Kara.

"Yes, midnight, not only, but they all sneaked out of the Professor's house on their tiptoes and snuck back into their houses."

"But I was watching, wasn't I, oh yes, I was," screeched Gladys.

"Oh, will you stop all that cackling," said Eve.

"I'm sure we can find out what happened because the boys are going to have another cup of tea, so they have something to stare at, and then they will start telling us what on earth is going on."

"Professor, I didn't expect you to be in a situation like this one," said Kara.

The Professor cleared his voice.

"Well, ladies of the jury, I think I can explain," he said as he nodded his head to thank Eve for the extra tea.

"WELL THEN, EXPLAIN!!" yelled Gladys.

Tobia stared at her. He had never seen this side of her. It was actually quite scary.

"Yes, well, where shall I begin."

"From the beginning," said Kara as she sat on the floor cross-legged, quite interested in what was about to be told.

The Professor told how Slumber had noticed Tobia escape and how they had decided to see what he was up to and had gone into the woods to find out.

"THE WOODS??" said the ladies in unison.

There was an old legend about the woods that claimed that anybody who went in would never, or hardly ever, come back out. The story said there was a sort of magical power in the trees that would not let you in or let you out. They say that long long ago, the land had been flooded once and to cross it, an old bard had used a magical potion which he had dropped into the water. When the water had dried up, the trees had remained enchanted, for their roots had drunk up all the potion and they had taken over the land in anger and revenge. That could be the reason for which the camper had been stuck in the mud and left there. No one ever dared to go there. It was unbelievable that Tobia actually had.

The thing about legends is that you never know if they are true but you never really want to find out if they are.

"Yes, ladies, the woods," he replied, slightly irritated.

He continued by telling them that they found Tobia in a camper stuck in a sort of lake in the middle of the woods.

He purposely omitted the information about their getting stuck in the mud and the dancing and the running and all those sorts of details that would be of no interest to the ladies of the group. Besides, guys have to stick up for each other, you know.

"A camper??" Kara asked.

"Stuck in the mud?" Gladys said.

"In the woods?" Elsa asked.

"Yes, that's what I said, but I must put an emphasis on the fact that we still do not know why Tobia was in the camper, how he found it, or why he was in it, in the middle of the night, I might add. Sorry, dear lad, I would have preferred talking about it in a more gentleman way in another type of environment."

"I know," said Tobia as he took a deep breath.

"You KNOW!! What on earth are you talking about? You know. You've got quite bit of explaining dear mole," yelled Gladys.

"I think it's about time you calm down, if not to SHUT UP now and let the poor guy speak," said Eve trying to keep her patience even though her instinct would have been to pluck all of her sister's feathers out!

"Ok everybody, let poor Tobia talk," said Kara.

Tobia started explaining how he had gone for a walk to find flowers to put in his house (actually to give Gladys, but that wasn't interesting right this moment). Since it was a sunny day, he thought going into the woods would have been nice. He remembered from the stories that nothing had ever happened in the daytime. He hadn't brought his compass with him, so he got lost and found himself in the middle of the woods after hours of walking in circles, in front of a white camper stuck in the mud. His curiosity got the best of him and he found some wood and managed to climb into the camper. He said it was so cosy and homey, he fell asleep on the bed and woke up sometime later just before it started getting dark.

He continued saying that he had gone to the camper every day for a week, bringing wooden planks to make the entering and exiting easier. It had become a secret escape for him, even though, he had to be honest, he always had to get lost to find it. Slumber and the Professor looked up at each other. Now that they thought about it, they too had gotten lost to find it. Tobia told them how he had gone through the fence to make the escape easier and so that he wouldn't have to walk in front of Slumber's house all the time, waiting for him not to be there, so as not to see him.

He explained how he was silently reading a book when he suddenly heard some sounds outside (he omitted the dancing in his boxers part, on purpose, obviously) and found the two intruders hugging and staring at him.

"That could have been avoided," said the Professor in a serious voice.

"I agree," said Slumber.

"Well, anyway, we all came back together, had a warm cup of tea at the Professor's, and went to bed. What time it was, I do not recall." As he finished his story, he sat back down, exhausted and, well, we can say, slightly worried.

What happened after was quite a tornado of words, cackling and questions and ifs and should haves and all the words just lifted in a tornado above their heads, until they finally fell down and everybody was silent again.

The plan

That Sunday morning had been quite an exhausting morning for our friends at the farm and at the end of the discussion, Kara had decided that it was best if everyone went back to their rooms and houses to stay on their own a little bit and think about what had been said. Everyone's head was so full that they all thought it was a good idea and so it happened that each one went back to their houses to think about the morning and relax a little.

The three friends, Professor, Slumber, and Tobia went back to their houses and simply fell asleep on their beds. All this chatter and all those questions and yelling had gotten into their heads.

They were not used to things being so complicated. Life was usually much simpler than that. They fell into a long sleep; in all honesty, they quite deserved it.

The hens went back upstairs and sat in their living room for five minutes just staring at each other in awe. After which, with nothing to say for the first time, each went into her own room and collapsed.

It had been an exhausting morning for them all, Kara thought as she too lay on her bed. They were not used to all that anger and confusion and yelling at each other. Life on the farm was always full of happiness and love. It was strange to feel what they were feeling. She pulled her woolly blanket over her and fell asleep with Pebbles.

The farm was silent. Nothing moved for a long time. So long, they actually skipped lunch and just kept on sleeping. Drops started to fall on the roof and they got stronger and stronger. Rain was the best thing for thinking, even better if accompanied by a nice warm cup of tea.

Slowly each one started to get up.

The Professor lit his pipe and made himself some toast and butter with a nice cup of tea. He sat at his table, thinking and puffing.

Tobia did the same thing. He drank a cup of tea and then he snuggled back into bed, thinking about what had happened. He was quite sad. His adventure had come to an end. Nothing bad had actually happened but he just felt disappointed about the way things had gone over all. He finally had something special, something for himself, and it was over now.

Slumber got up and put a warm jumper on. It was always a little colder on this side of the farm. He too sat on the bed thinking it all over, quite disappointed in it all.

The ladies, on the other hand, got up one at a time and sat around their little living room. None of them had much to say so they just commented on how hard the rain was coming down.

Kara walked down the stairs and went into the kitchen. She lit the fire, took a piece of cake, made a fresh pot of tea, and sat on the armchair with a cosy blanket on her knees, thinking.

The barn door was open and she could see the rain. She loved watching and hearing the sound of rain. She had woken up with a plan in mind and was ready to tell her friends as soon as they would all appear. The air was full of disappointment and she couldn't bear for her friends to feel that way. She was determined to make a change and turn this all into the beginning of an exciting adventure.

The clock struck five times, tea time. Kara was sure everyone would soon start arriving and so it was. The hens came downstairs. They had a sort of guiltiness about them, especially Gladys, who wished she hadn't yelled so much and been so hard on Tobia. He hadn't done anything wrong at the end of the day, he had just gone on an adventure on his own and her anger, now that she thought about it, was just because she had been worried. Sometimes when we are really angry, things don't come out just right and we take it out on people just because we haven't understood what the bottom feeling is. Now she knew, and she was determined to apologize to everyone, especially Tobia.

He was actually the next one to come in. He took off his raincoat, shook off the rain, and sat down on the sofa. He was wearing the high collar jumper Gladys had made him. They exchanged looks and smiled at each other.

The Professor walked in with his polka dot umbrella, took his boots off, and took position on his rocking chair. "Good evening, everyone," he said in a serious tone.

"Good evening, Professor," they all replied in unison.

"Well, the gang is punctual as always, on the dot for tea," said Slumber as he walked in, but nobody replied, the general mood was submissive and silent.

Kara served everyone a cup of tea and a slice of leftover cake. She took the blackboard she used for studying and placed it in the middle of the room so that everyone could see it.

"Hello everyone, before we start, there are a couple of things I would like to say to you all. Firstly, I'm very sorry about how things went, about this morning. We are a small family and we are not used to arguing. I hope it will never happen again. We are used to being there for one another and not against one another. On the other hand, sometimes discussions are good because they make you realize how much you care about someone, where you went wrong, and what you can adjust so that it doesn't happen again. Having said this, I can feel the energy of this room as you all can, and I would like it to change and return to the way it was.

"There is no reason to be sad or disappointed, these things happen and it is nobody's fault, and if you really think about it, nobody did anything wrong after all."

"I agree," commented the Professor.

"I would like to say something," said Gladys.

"Go ahead," said Kara.

She cleared her voice. "Firstly, I would like to apologize to everyone for my yelling and cackling, it was not nice at all. I'd like to say sorry to my sisters for my rude replies but I would especially like to say sorry to Tobia for the way I spoke to him, it was unkind and not nice at all. You did nothing wrong, Tobia, and I'm sorry I spoiled your secret adventure for you."

"Thank you, Gladys, I appreciate your kind words and thank you, Kara," Tobia said in a thin voice.

There was a three-minute moment where hens and mole and Kara hugged. Slumber and the Professor watched while sipping on their tea.

"When I went up to bed this morning, I realised that we can turn this negative start into something positive and actually make it a farm adventure. " said Kara

"How's that?" questioned the Professor.

"Well, if Tobia doesn't mind, I thought we could go into the woods and look for the camper and bring it back home and then call the police to pick it back up!"

"Oh, what an Adventure," said the hens all together in excited and scared voices.

Slumber raised his eyebrows and looked over at the Professor who exchanged the glance by raising his eyebrows too.

"Well, if I may," said Tobia as he went over to the kitchen table to get yesterday's paper. "I actually don't think we have to give it back." He opened the newspaper to the page he was looking for.

The Professor sat up. His curiosity had been piqued. Slumber too started paying more attention.

"I found a picture of the camper in the paper. It says that the owners gave up on it because they cannot remove it from the mud. They authorize anyone who finds it to keep it."

A sudden "HOOORAY" filled the room. Even the Professor and Slumber jumped up and they all started cheering and hugging each other!

"Congratulations, old chap," said the Professor as he shook Tobia's hand.

"Silence, everyone," said Kara as they all sat back down.

The air had changed and the farm had found its cheer and enthusiasm back again. As Kara looked around, she saw all of her friends smiling. A sort of excitement for a new adventure had entered into their lives again.

"Now what we need is a plan, everyone! A plan to go and get ourselves a camper!" said Kara in an excited voice.

"What will we do with it, and how will we bring it back here?" asked Eve. She wasn't quite an adventurous hen but she was happy everything had gone back to the way it used to be.

"I don't know, honestly. I just like the fact that we can all go on an adventure together. I think that we could use it to go on new adventures all together, travel around, and see new places. I've always wanted to travel and see different things. Don't get me wrong – I love this place, the farm, our lives together – but I've always loved the idea of going somewhere new. Every time my parents and Richard leave, I wish I could go too, so I travel in my head and imagine new things and people. This could be the chance I've been waiting for. It's a little home but you can travel with it and stop whenever you want, eat, sleep in it. It just sounds so exciting, as if it was the missing part of my dreams. It's like they're all coming to life!!"

Everyone in the room could feel Kara's excitement and that made them excited too, but one fact remained: The woods.

To do this, they would have to go into the woods.

"That's why we have to put out heads together and plan it all out."

"I'll make some more tea," said Elsa. "Is stew alright for everyone?" she asked. "I can heat it up and we can eat it as we plan."

"Perfect," they all replied together.

Vegetable stew and a plan was just the sort of evening the Professor and Slumber would call "the perfect combination."

Kara drew a quick map of the farm and the woods on the board.

As she did that, a shiver went up their backs.

"Professor, I think this next part is up to you and the guys. None of us have ever been there so we have no idea about the whereabouts," said Kara as she sat down on the carpet in front of the fire with a bowl of stew and a blanket on her back.

The night was starting to get quite chilly and Tobia helped Eve close the farm door. They were all gathered around the fire like a family, listening to the Professor.

"Well, hmmmm," he started as he cleared his throat. "I suppose the best way out would be from the front gate, don't you agree, Tobia?"

"Yes, I think that's best," he replied. "After which, we have to 'get lost' in the woods. I've been going back and forth and there is no real way to get there. I think the best path would be the one I always take and then we just take it from there."

"What time will we leave?" asked Gladys.

"Well," Slumber pitched in. "I think it shouldn't be too late because then it'll be too dark and scary to get back."

"Oh dear," whispered Eve.

"Around four?" asked Kara.

"Yes, four o'clock would be perfect. We have to wear something warm. We should bring torches and some utensils to get the camper out," continued Slumber.

"Yes, we must bring ropes and wood and maybe some gas to put in the engine," said Tobia.

"Well thought out, Tobia. What about the keys? Did you find any, to start the car with, I mean?" asked the Professor.

"Yes, they just left them there. There is also food in the cabinets in case of an emergency."

"That's my field," Elsa said. "My sisters and I will organize some baskets of food."

"Nothing too heavy, ladies, we must travel as light as possible in case we need to escape," said Slumber.

"Escape?" said Elsa. "Oh dear."

"Well, I know, it's not such a manly thing to say, but it does get quite scary in those woods as soon as the sun goes down."

"Well, couldn't we go in the morning then?" said Kara.

"I suppose we could, what do you think, Tobia?" said Slumber.

"Well, I guess. I never have, but we could try."

"Perfect, we leave next Saturday, at around 10:00 a.m. I'll get up early to do my homework. In the meantime, the girls can pack some food and we'll meet here and leave. What do you think?"

Someone had to say what they were all thinking but no one dared to.

Until suddenly Eve spoke out.

"Well, I think this is the most stupid idea in the world. Sorry, Kara, I love the fact that your dream will come true but does anybody here realize that all our lives could be at risk? Ever since I was a chick, my father would tell me stories of the woods and we were all prohibited to leave the farm. I remember when I was small, I would spend hours looking at the woods from here and imagining horrible things happening to me and now all of a sudden, we just all agree to go in!! Are you all out of your minds? It's a miracle Tobia came back from that stupid adventure of his! He himself said it was scary to go in and he didn't know how to go in and out! Do you realize how lucky we are to have him here sound and safe? And now, just as if we were having toast with jam we say, 'Ok, let's go see if we can go die in the woods and never come back!' Yeah, I couldn't wait for anything better to happen to me than disappear in some dark enchanted wood full of angry trees! You all have lost your minds!"

The room suddenly fell silent. No one dared to sip on the soup. Eve was right and they all knew it.

"Eve," said Slumber as he stood up to speak. "I think I speak for everyone here if I say that we all agree with you and are as scared as you are. I must admit those woods are scary and when the Professor and I went in, it was dark and mouldy and everything was just as it had been described to me as a pup. But I was not alone. The Professor was with me and I felt stronger that way. I knew that I had someone I could count on and I knew I had to get Tobia out of there as fast as possible. I wasn't showing it but I was scared as hell."

"Well said," whispered the Professor.

"But you know what, Kara has been taking care of me, of us, since she was small. She has been there to play with us, to cure us, to feed us and to stand up for us. She has never ever asked for anything in return. She has always put everyone else first, including her parents and brother. She has never gone out of this farm apart for on the bus to school and has never asked anything of us. So, if now for once I can help make her dream come true, I am willing to do so without thinking twice. We will all be together, we will take care of each other, and we will come home safe, I promise. Dreams are made to come true; Kara has given me everything a dog like me could have ever wanted and I will be by her side all the way." He sat down on the sofa and wiped his tears away before anyone could see them.

The Professor patted him on the back as did Tobia. "Well said, old chap."

We're in," they said in unison, glancing at the sisters to see what they were thinking.

Elsa and Gladys looked at each other. They had a lump in their throat and drank to make it go down.

"Well," said Gladys as she cleared her own throat. "I understand what Eve is saying and honestly, I remember growing up with the stories of the woods and I am not a very courageous person so going there does scare me quite a bit. On the other hand, I agree with Slumber that if we are all together, it will be easier and that if this is to make Kara's dream come true, then I suppose I could find some courage somewhere inside me."

Elsa looked around. She was next. They were all staring at her and she felt a little nervous. "I-I...Oh dear, I'm scared too. I was very worried when I listened to the guys talking and I honestly hoped that it was all over and done with and that we could all go back to our lovely daily life, it's just so perfect...I do agree about dreams. I think that we have to reach for them and try and make them come true otherwise, life wouldn't make much sense. I agree that Kara should have the chance to make hers come true and we are the only ones that can do that for her. Oh dear, I suppose that if I have all of you around me, I can do this, although I am terribly frightened."

Eve stared at them all and ran up to her room and slammed the door.

No one spoke. The room was silent.

Kara sighed and put down her bowl. She too went upstairs, leaving everyone feeling terribly guilty and confused.

The next few hours were incredibly tense. Slowly each one went back to their rooms and houses and silence filled the air. Only Pebbles moved. Looking around, she could feel that something was not quite right, so she slowly made her way up to Kara's room. The door was slightly open and Kara was lying on her bed, staring at the ceiling.

"Oh Pebbles," she said as she grabbed the cat and stroked her. "Maybe I'm just asking too much of everyone," she said. "They are right, life here is perfect, but sometimes I think it's too perfect and I would just love some adventure in my life. When I heard about the camper, I couldn't believe it. You know when you start getting bubbles in your stomach like something incredible is about to happen? Well, that's how I felt, like it was something magical had come my way. Maybe I should go there on my own and just keep everyone out of it. I mean, the guys did it, Tobia went there on his own... Oh, I don't know, Pebbles, what should I do?"

Pebbles looked at her and licked her tears. They lay together, waiting for an answer to arrive from somewhere.

In the meantime, Elsa and Gladys went to knock on Eve's door.

"May we come in, dear?" they asked in unison.

"If you really have to," replied Eve. She was lying on her bed with her wings crossed. The sisters sat on the bed and leaned down to hug her.

"We both agree with you," said Elsa. "I'm so scared, I think I lost a couple of feathers when I heard the whole thing, and I went back in time when Dad would tell us those terrible stories. I remember sometimes I had nightmares about the trees coming to get me."

"Oh, me too," said Gladys.

"Then why?? Why do you want to go along with this plan?" Eve asked in tears.

"We don't," said Gladys, "but we have to, Slumber is right. Kara has given us the perfect life, living on this farm and being all together makes us the luckiest chickens in the world. I couldn't have dreamt of a better life, but Kara deserves to have at least one dream come true. She has never spoken about this wish of hers and honestly, I thought she was perfectly happy here, but evidently inside of her, she's sad. I think that every time her parents and Richard go away, she is in pain. I think it hurts her to be here all alone. Even though she's not really alone, she is alone inside."

"Remember all the times she helped us out," said Elsa. "Remember when we were chicks and she would spoon feed us because we were too small? And all the times she would lay down on the grass and let us jump all over her? Remember her giggles and how she would make us fly by putting us on her knees and lifting them up?"

They laughed; Eve smiled. "Yes, I remember."

"Well, don't you think that such a sweet and lovely girl deserves a chance to be really happy?"

"I think she does," continued Gladys. "I'm so scared but I think that somehow if we stick together, we can do it, as a team."

Eve looked at her sisters, she loved them so much and she didn't want to lose them, but they were right. Kara was a special little girl and they had to make her wish come true. In some way.

"Ok," she said. "But promise me we will come back together."

"I hope so, Eve, I certainly hope so."

The three sisters hugged. It was a long time since this had happened and there was a sort of magic in that hug, it was a love hug, one of those hugs that tightens your heart.

"Kara is in her room, love. If you want to go and talk to her, we'll wait for you in the living room," said Elsa as they accompanied her to the corridor.

"Eve, just speak from your heart and everything will be ok," said Gladys, stroking her sisters' feathers.

Eve slowly and silently went up to Kara's room. She could see her with Pebbles on her tummy, just lying there on her side with her eyes closed.

"May I come in, Kara?" she whispered

"Eve, yes, of course you can. I'm so sorry, Eve," said Kara. "I never meant to put any of you in danger, it was just a silly idea."

"No, it wasn't," replied Eve, sitting on the bed next to her. "I was looking into your dream closet. I mean, I believe we all have a closet where we put our dreams, but we just keep them there and don't quite dare to look inside because they're just dreams, but you opened it and saw that it was staring you right in the face, as if it had come out to find you."

"Yes, that's exactly how I felt," said Kara, looking down.

"Well, I'm not going to be the chicken to stop that from happening," said Eve with a giggle.

"Oh, Eve, thank you so much, I will never forget this, ever."

They hugged as tight as ever.

"Kara, you're choking me," said Eve in a whistle of a voice. "You're going to make chicken for dinner if you keep doing that."

"Oh dear!! Sorry!"

They burst out in a loud laugh. Elsa and Gladys ran inside and hugged the two of them.

"Where did you pop out from?" said Kara.

"Oh, you know us, we're always around." Gladys winked. Together they burst out in a hearty laugh and Pebbles sat on the bed watching this crazy sight of three chickens lying on the floor on top of a little girl.

"Let's go down and tell the others," said Kara.

The hens followed her, cackling away, but when they came down stairs, the room was empty and the men were gone.

"Now where on earth have those three gone to?" said Gladys in a snotty tone.

"Oh, probably being boys, they couldn't handle all the emotional stuff and went to hide somewhere. Let's look at the Professor's house."

Sure enough, there they were. They could see a light from the window and the three of them smoking away and laughing around the table.

"Good evening, gentlemen," said Gladys as she opened the door.

Tobia dropped his cigar on the floor and drank down his cider.

"Watch out, dear, don't step on it, might burn your precious feet," said Gladys with a wink.

"Make space, women coming in with a plan," said Elsa as she and the girls sat around the table.

"Bring out the bottle, let's have a round of cider, chaps, we've got a plan to talk about."

From outside, Pebbles watched as they all drank together and laughed around the Professor's table, looking over a big map.

That's the magic of love, when you let it out, it grabs onto you and gets contagious...Pebbles went away, leaving the gang to their evening in search of Granny's warm lap to lie on.

They finished up their drinks and said goodnight and went off to bed.

The mood was exciting, each one thinking about this new adventure. Even though fear was still in the background, something inside them had brought courage out as well, and that was enough for a day like this.

"Goodnight, Kara, sleep tight and God bless you. This farm wouldn't be the same without you. You make this family what it is and we are so lucky to have you," said Elsa as they went up to bed.

"No, it wouldn't be the same without any of us."

"Sleep tight and don't go to bed too late," she said with a wink.

She knew the hens would gather round and chat, even if there was a week ahead.

The girls gathered round the fire; Eve looked under the sink.

"It's at the back, behind the onions," said Elsa.

"Here it is, lemon cider, just the thing we need tonight," she said as she got the tiny coffee cups and poured a sip for her sisters.

"Well, ladies, let's cheer to dreams coming true."

They cheered to that and laughed.

The rain had stopped and the air was chilly. Three lights shone in the night. Around the fireplace, the hens organised how to keep everyone well fed and warm.

On the top floor, Kara's bedside table lamp was on. She was putting on her pyjamas.

What a perfect ending to a terrible beginning, she thought. *Sometimes it's best to find the other side of things and make them positive.* As she thought about the camper, she fell asleep with the sounds of her friends laughing in the background.

The field trip

Monday started with a beautiful rainbow in the sky. The rain had stopped and the sun was out again. They all took it as a good omen. Kara hopped off to school and the farm activities went on as usual but with an exciting buzz in the air. The week never seemed to end. That happens sometimes when we can't wait for something to happen. It seems as if time has stopped, doesn't it? At dinner, there was only talk about the hows and ifs and quite a busy organization of the field trip, or better the "woods trip."

Finally, Saturday morning did arrive and there was a big hassle in the house. While Elsa put the kettle on, Gladys made the sandwiches and Eve put everything in the backpacks. They had decided to bring those instead of baskets because they were easier to carry. One was for the food; another had the first aid kit and blankets and socks and shirts in case someone got stuck in the mud and had to change. I must say that Elsa was quite an organized chicken. She had thought of everything in case anything happened.

The Professor showed up looking quite professional. He had a raincoat on with an elegant silk scarf, tracking boots, his pipe (obviously) and a belt with all sorts of instruments on it. Tobia and Slumber showed up looking just about the same. They wore high collar shirts, rain jackets, and backpacks. Tobia had put on his detective hat. He had quite the important look about him. I must say that the sisters looked quite funny. They had put they woolly dresses on, their scarves on their heads, and Gladys had one of her special scarves around her neck – to protect her voice, obviously. Eve had brought her canvases in her back pack and you could see a paintbrush sticking out of her backpack.

"What is that for?" asked Kara.

"Oh, it's a 'just in case.' I put in, just in case," replied the chicken.

"Well, everyone, here we are, has everyone had something to eat?"

"No," they replied in unison.

"Well, why not? We can't go without food in our stomach! Come on, everyone, let's have a bite. We can't leave Elsa's apple cake just sitting there, can we now? It seems quite rude to me."

"Oh, we certainly cannot," said the Professor as he sat down.

Elsa filled the cups of tea and everyone had a slice. Even though the cake was quite delicious, it didn't seem to go down so well. They were just too excited, and scared too, someone put the slices in their pocket and washed down the rest with some tea. In less than five minutes they were all outside, ready to go.

Kara looked at the Professor. They were the only two left at the table. "Well, I suppose we should go."

"I suppose," he replied, cutting himself another slice of cake.

They all started to walk away from the barn door. Kara locked it well and off they went.

It was the first time they had ever done something like this all together and their tummies had some sort of strange butterfly or two swimming in them.

"Ok everyone," said Kara in a loud voice as they all gathered around her in a circle. "Firstly, I want to thank everyone for being here and for supporting me on this adventure dream. It's very important for me to have my family around me and I will be forever grateful, I want you to know this." They all clapped.

"I also want to say that I am as scared as you all are, no one's talking about it but I know that we are all terrorized to go in there. I have faith in our guide Tobia and our men for they have already been there and have come back. Having said this, I think that the most important thing is to stick together. If we are together, we are strong. We have to support each other and be there for one another. I know we can do this and I'm sure we will come back successful. Let's do this, guys!!"

They all huddled up and hugged.

"Let go get ourselves a camper!" they yelled.

Tobia led the line. Behind him was the Professor and Slumber and behind them Kara, Elsa, and Gladys. Eve was the last in line. They closed the gate and stared at the farm, looked at each other, and held wings. It was a very long stare. Each one of them was leaving a part of themselves in that house and silently hoping to be back very very soon.

The sisters hadn't held wings since they were small but it felt pretty good in that moment. They smiled at each other, took a deep breath, and off they went...

The sun was shining but the Professor could see some dark clouds in the distance. He elbowed Slumber and nodded at them. Slumber looked back at him with a worried look. They hastened their pace.

"Everyone alright?" asked Kara.

There was a general humming noise which she took as a sort of yes. As they got closer to the woods, they all squished together. They looked like a sort of cannon ball with feathers walking into the woods.

As Tobia put his foot into the woods, he took a deep breath, and so did everyone else as they walked in. *Wow, these woods have such a strong power,* thought Kara as she turned around to make a quick count of everyone. "What now, Tobia?" she asked.

They were all standing there huddled up in a big ball staring up at the trees, which were staring down at them. Fear was the only word to describe the whole group at that moment in time. "Well, now we get lost," he replied in a wobbly voice.

"I think we went that way," said Slumber, sniffing the air.

"Do you? I think it was that way." The Professor pointed in the opposite direction.

"Well, that's lovely, isn't it?" Eve whispered to her sister.

"It's ok, Eve, we're supposed to get lost or we can't find it," Kara whispered back.

"I'm starting to think this was not such a good idea after all," whispered Elsa.

Kara was thinking the same thing, but she said nothing.

The woods were incredibly dark. The air smelt of mould and the trees were huge. Darkness was all around them and the wind started blowing. It was cold. The stillness was daunting. It was as if they had entered a different world. They could feel terror and their stomachs were as tight as a tiny stone. No one dared speak. They stuck together and walked in the mud, slowly and carefully as if every move could wake some mysterious owner that was just waiting to catch them and.... that thought was just too much...

The trees were immensely tall and stared down at them as if they were trespassers that had no right to be there. The bark of the tree was dark. There was a slight opening at the top of the tree which gave them enough light to see where they were going. It was all quite creepy.

After about an hour of going in circles and squares and triangles, there was still no sight of the camper.

"Let's stop and rest," said Elsa. "It's no use just walking around and getting dirty for nothing!"

"I agree, everyone, let's take a rest but let's stay close," Kara said in a sort of loud quiet voice.

They all sat on their backpacks for they didn't want to get any dirtier than they already were. With all the rain that had come down on the weekend, I must say there was quite a lot of mud. Kara helped Elsa pass out biscuits and a sip of warm herb tea, much appreciated by them all, obviously.

The three males sat together in a small circle, and the Professor pulled out a small bottle of something which he poured in their now empty glasses. "To getting lost," he said. They all toasted to that. "To getting lost and not going back without the camper," added Tobia in a quiet tone.

The atmosphere was starting to get a bit gloomy. The ladies were tired, and the men were disappointed and confused. To add to that, just above them sat a big fat black cloud which they obviously could not see because it was just above the tips of the trees. Kara was disappointed, for them, mostly. What if the legend is right? No one shall enter and no one shall leave. Had she brought her friends to a terrible end? She had wanted this adventure so much, she hadn't thought that it would be so scary and tiring and now maybe they had to go back without any luck, not only but maybe they would never get out at all! As this terrible thought entered her mind, she saw a large circle in the middle of the woods with a camper right in the middle of it! She couldn't believe it! Where had it come from? They had walked that way so many times in that hour!

"I found it," she yelled. "I found it."

The three men stood up and put their backpacks right on their backs and ran towards her, while the hens quickly put all the cups and cookies back in the bag. "A little help would be appreciated," yelled Eve, looking at the four, but just as she finished the sentence, she felt a drop of water on her head, then another and another!

"RUUUUUUUUN!" she screamed, cackling as chickens do.

Kara grabbed the backpacks and they all ran towards the camper.

The trees had lowered their heads and the water was now allowed to pour into the forest right on top of our friends.

"The planks, the planks!" yelled Tobia.

"Where?" yelled Slumber.

"Behind the tree, behind you."

"AHHHHHHHHHHHHHHH," screamed the ladies as the water came down stronger and stronger. They screamed lounder and louder and the sound echoed all through the woods. Fear took over and panic was everywhere.

The three guys, with the help of Kara, put the planks from the land to the camper door and Tobia ran towards the door to open it.

"Run, ladies, run, everybody come in!" He had to yell because the rain was making so much noise and coming down so hard, he couldn't hear nor see anyone. He wished he had never found this camper!

Suddenly Gladys appeared. "Oh, you are my hero," she said and gave him a quick peck on the cheek. He froze for a split second in awe and wonder then he yelled again, "Let's go everyone, inside."

They all scrambled in and he slammed the camper door. They all stood still in utter silence as the rain poured down without pity. They were in the middle of a thunderstorm, in the middle of the enchanted woods.

The magic camper

Tobia scrambled around and put a small light on. He turned around and locked the door. *You never know,* he thought.

"Woooooooooow," they all said together.

Tobia smiled, satisfied. "It's lovely, isn't it? I dare say magical," he whispered.

"Oh, it is just lovely," said Elsa. "It's just like a little house."

"It IS a little house," replied Tobia. "A little house on wheels which you can move and go places and see things and enjoy the world."

As the light shone, they began to see the shapes of things. There was a little table with two little sofas on each side. Elsa sat on it as soon as she realized what it was, as did Eve.

Above their heads on top of the driver's seat was a big double bed and behind them two bunk beds.

"Oh, this IS lovely," said Kara. "I've never seen anything quite like this."

"Yes, I must admit it is quite a well thought out area," said the Professor as he looked around, studying the shapes and their uses.

"Quite so," responded Slumber. "Well done, lad," he said, as he patted Tobia on the back.

"Welcome to OUR camper," said Tobia in a proud voice.

"Oh, look at all the cabinets," said Elsa. "And what is THAT!?"

"Oh, that's the kitchen," replied Tobia. "Look, if I lift this, there's the stove under, and under here there are the pots and pans. Over there in that cabinet are the plates and right over here," he said as he opened a drawer, "the cutlery."

"OH this is just pure magic!" squeaked Elsa as she looked around in awe.

"What about this little door? What's in here?" asked Kara.

They all stood there in disbelief. It was a fridge! An actual fridge in a car!

"Oh, my goodness, what an incredible place this is," said Eve.

"Look at this," Tobia said as he opened the door behind them.

There it was, complete with washbasin and toilet and shower, a beautiful blue and white bathroom!

"I don't believe it," said the Professor.

Slumber opened a cabinet on top of the fridge and saw it was a storage space for clothes and there was an even bigger cupboard right next to the bunkbeds with a lovely mirror on the door!

"Incredible," they all thought, as they looked around them.

"Where is the driver's seat?" asked Slumber.

"Right behind that curtain," replied the mole.

Slumber drew aside the curtain and found himself in heaven, a huge driver's seat with another right next to it. He shut it right away because outside the sight was terrifying.

Rain was pouring down. The thunderstorm had taken over. From the outside, it was quite a freaky scene. All you could see was a muddy camper sunk in the mud and huge trees with their tips hanging down as if they were peering inside.

"WELL, WELL," said the Professor. He was quite surprised and pleased and satisfied and curious all at the same time. The rain got stronger and stronger.

"I think we're going to have to stay here for the night," said Kara.

That was the worst thing she could have said, everyone was so terror-stricken. They stood petrified. Eve almost fainted and Gladys sat down. Elsa held on to the table. She thought she was going to have a heart attack. The professor lit his pipe and puffed on it so strongly, it was like he was making smoke signals.

"We'll be ok," said Tobia. "I've been here before. As long as we stay inside and lock everything up, we'll be ok."

"Of course we will," said Slumber. "We're inside the camper and no one can hurt us." As soon as he said that, the camper shook hard and they all screamed! The shaking didn't stop. It just kept getting stronger and stronger. It felt like they were being tipped over.

"We're gonna dieeeee!" screamed Elsa. And they all screamed again. It felt like an earthquake. The noise was getting louder and louder and things were just falling everywhere. They all scrambled to the floor and held on to whatever they could find. "Hold on, everyone," screamed Kara. At that precise moment, a thunder bolt cracked right next to them. It was so incredibly loud, they all jumped.

"We've been hit," yelled Gladys. "The monsters are coming to get us. Heeeelp," she screamed.

Everyone panicked and screeched. The camper was a big mess and everyone was just lying on top of each other trying to hold on to someone, something...to life itself. Tobia was holding onto the front seat and Gladys was under him, screaming and shaking. Kara and Eve were huddled together under the table and Elsa was rocking back and forth. She could not find anything to hold on to.

Finally, the Professor managed to catch her and she clung to his legs. Slumber sat on the driver's seat, bouncing from side to side, as if he was on a roller coaster ride.

Something outside was bouncing the camper from side to side. They heard a strong roar, like horrible laughter. As the rain got stronger, so did the shaking. Mud squirted all over the windows and the camper started lifting and falling. The trees were having fun trying to get those tiny beings out of there.

Inside the camper, everyone just held on as tight as possible. No one spoke or yelled anymore. They had been found and the legend was a reality. The trees were alive and very angry.

Suddenly the rain stopped. The camper rose up into the air. "That's it, it's oveeer, we're deaaaad," yelled the chickens.

And then it banged hard into the mud.

SLAAAAAAAAAM! They all hit the ceiling then bounced back onto the floor.

Stop.

Nothing.

Silence.

The camper was still.

No one spoke, everyone held their breath, was it over?

No, it wasn't. They rose again and again and slammed down another two or three times. The slams and bangs were so hard, it seemed as though it was going to break. It was the worst nightmare they had ever lived and they would never forget it, if they got out of there alive, that was.

In an instant, it was all quiet again. The trees lifted their branches as if they had given up, the wind stopped blowing, everything and everyone was still.

"It's over," said Kara and she started crying.

"Is everyone ok?" asked Slumber.

"Yes," said the Professor, "but I am definitely too old for something like this."

It was funny but no one had the energy to laugh.

They all picked themselves up. The camper was a disaster. The lovely home had become a mess, cups and plates and blankets scattered everywhere.

"Thank goodness we were inside," said Eve. "Imagine what would have happened if we hadn't found this camper."

"No, let's not," replied the Professor, quite serious and worried.

"Is anyone hurt?" asked Slumber.

"Bruised and I've got a terrible headache," said Elsa.

"Me too," replied Tobia.

"The important thing is that no one broke anything. I think we should just find a place to lie down and sleep or rest our bodies at least. Elsa, is there still something to eat?"

"Eat?? How can you think of food!"

"Slumber is right," said Kara lifting herself up. "We must think of getting back up, slowly. Let's clean up as much as we can. I don't think any of us will sleep much but we can try now that everything seems silent. I'm so sorry, everyone, this is my fault. I brought us out here for my stupid dream and could have gotten us killed."

"Dear girl," said the Professor, "we chose to come here and honestly nobody could have known this was going to happen. Sometimes legends are just old stories made up. We could never have imagined that these trees were actually alive! The important thing now is that we are all ok. The camper has protected us so far, and I must say it has quite a sturdy structure. Let's get some rest and get out of here as soon as light comes back."

They all started putting things back into the once lovely cabinets. The window were full of mud and outside it was still dark. Gladys pulled the curtain up and they lit a small candle so as not to get too much attention from the outside.

Elsa and the girls looked in the cabinets to see what they could find. They found a lovely red polka dot tablecloth, which they lay on the table, then they found blankets and big fluffy yellow comforters to put on the beds. Eve and Gladys worked on the beds as Elsa started to take things out of the backpack and place them on the table. *What a lovely place this is*, she thought with a big smile on her face. Kara and the boys looked at all the buttons and their uses and tried to understand all the commands at the front.

After not so long, the table was set with sandwiches of all types and a bottle of water and napkins. "Elsa, what would we do without you?" said Kara "Thank you, the beds look so soft and cozy. Girls, I must say, you did a perfect job!"

"You certainly did," said the three males in unison.

They finished their dinner in silence and started to think about sleeping. They were all extremely tired and their bodies felt all mushy whooshy from all the banging and hitting.

"Ok, well, how many beds are there?" said Kara. "How shall we sleep?"

"Well, there are four beds and we are seven," said Tobia.

"I thought maybe Kara and the girls can sleep in the double bed upstairs and the Professor and Slumber can sleep on the bunkbeds and I can sleep on the sofa."

"Sounds perfect. Let's help Elsa put things away, then we can take turns for the toilet, get changed, and go to bed," Kara said. "I know this is a stupid question but how does the toilet work exactly? Does everything drop on the ground outside?"

"No such thing as a stupid question," said the Professor, clearing out his voice and puffing on his pipe.

"Tobia and I were talking about it earlier on our walk here. There is a sort of tank that collects it all and then you just throw it away," replied Slumber.

"I wish I hadn't known," said Eve. "That kind of takes all the romance out of things, doesn't it?"

They laughed. "I suppose it does," said Kara.

"Well, having said that, ladies first," said the Professor as he opened the bathroom door to let the first girl in.

"That'd be me, if you don't mind," said Kara.

"No, no, go ahead, dear," the girls replied, quite embarrassed.

None of them had ever slept together in the same room so it was quite new to them all, sharing beds and toilets and being so tight, but I guess it was also what gave them the sense of family and brotherhood that they were all feeling.

The Professor pulled out a set of cards from his special belt and the guys started playing as the ladies got ready for bed.

"Are you guys up for a game? It helps to get our heads off things a little, make them feel normal."

"Why does this table dangle like this?" asked the Professor as his elbow moved up and down. "I suppose it's gotten quite a slamming!"

"Hmmm," said Slumber. "Let's see, maybe something is loose."

"Well, take a look at this," he said and they all popped their heads under the table. There was a strange sort of mechanism which seemed to be to holding the table.

"Oh well, try moving that piece."

"Ok, now lift."

Off came the table. Right in that moment, Kara came out of the bathroom and saw the three of them with a table in their hands.

"Oh dear, no more breakfast table," she said.

The chickens looked down to see what was going on.

"Oh no, it's not quite like that," said Tobia. "I think we've found something." They searched around the sofa to see if there were any clues and indeed there were, they discovered that there was a perfect spot to put the table on and the sofa mattresses filled the space on top of it and there it was! The table had transformed into another bed!

There was a loud applause from the upstairs.

"Tobia, your bed is bigger than what we had expected!" said Slumber.

"Oh, there is an extra comforter in the cupboards next to the beds," said Gladys. "Now we know what that was for, I suppose we must be ready for all sorts of surprises in this little house!"

"Quite excellent," remarked the Professor in a satisfied tone.

"Now off to bed everyone. Goodnight. I'm very pleased you are all here with me," remarked Tobia

"It's nicer to do things together, isn't it?" said Kara. "And I must say we are quite a team."

"Good night, *see you tomorrow*," said the hens as they closed their eyes (all except for one).

One by one they went under the soft yellow covers. Rain dropped on the roof of the camper. Each drop brought terror back into their stomachs and they looked around to see if something was about to happen. But it didn't and slowly they each started to fall asleep. The woods fell asleep and silence surrounded the camper. It was a very strange silence because it didn't really feel like silence. It was as if they were being watched.

Gladys quietly came down from the stairs and snuck into Tobia's bed. They hugged each other and fell asleep...just like everyone else.

The next morning Kara opened her eyes and didn't quite know where she was. That happens sometimes when you wake up in a different place, it takes a minute or so for your head to connect to the difference. Her body was in pain and she had bruises everywhere which reminded her of what had happened. She rose up quickly to see if everyone was there and ok. As she looked down from the bed, she saw Elsa tiptoeing around the camper, getting breakfast ready on the table.

The boys must have made it back into a table again. How clever, she thought. She heard some voices outside and noticed that there was a little window where her bed was. She moved the curtains and saw Slumber and Tobia outside on the planks going back and forth with their raincoats on. There was quite a bit of wind, which wasn't bad because it would help dry the mud.

Gladys was sitting on the passenger seat while the Professor was very seriously managing buttons behind the steering wheel.

"Eve dear," whispered Kara. "It's time to get up."

"Yes, what? Who are you? Oh, Kara, yes, the camper. Ahhhhh," she yelled in a confused state of mind. "That's ok."

Kara laughed. "It happened to me too. We're safe. It's morning. We must have all fallen asleep fast, and thank goodness nothing bad happened again."

She left Eve in bed to get back to herself as she went down the stairs.

"Good morning, Professor."

"Good morning, Kara, did you sleep well?"

"I most certainly did," she said. "Yes, I think we all did. It's ten o'clock already and we still have to have breakfast."

"Well, I didn't think we would have fallen asleep but I believe our bodies were under shock and needed rest." He smiled, giving the girl a pat on the back.

Breakfast was announced by Elsa who had laid cookies and pieces of chocolate cake on the table. "Unfortunately, the tea is cold, so we have nothing to drink except for water," she said.

"That's quite alright, Elsa, you spoiled us with such a lovely breakfast."

"Nonsense," said Slumber as he pulled out a small pot and poured the left-over tea in it. "This is a working kitchen," he said as he turned the fire on to heat the tea up.

"Well, I'll be darned," said Elsa, super happy.

So, there they were, cozy, with their chocolate cake slice and a small glass of warm tea, all around the table.

Tobia came in and shut the door behind him. "We have a problem," he said as he grabbed a slice of cake. "We cmmmt gmm ammwherrmm."

"Maybe swallow the cake first," said Gladys. "It's not polite to speak while you eat."

"And quite disgusting too," added Eve.

"Sorry," he said "I was saying, we have a problem."

"Yes, we got that part," said Eve.

"Oh. We can't get out of here, we are terribly stuck and if we ever do get unstuck, how will we go back to the farm??!"

"Well, no need to panic," replied the Professor. "We are stuck and it won't be easy to get out of the mud, which is the reason the camper is here without its original owners in the first place. Actually, now I can quite understand why they left it here, I would have done the same!! As far as getting to the farm, I found an alternative road, which is probably the one that brought the owners here. It's right behind us and should lead us to the main road and then back to the farm."

"Well, I'll tell you something, Professor, in the week I was here, I never found a road for a car. I always came back by foot. I looked everywhere for the road that brought me here and it is nowhere to be seen," said Tobia with an irritated voice.

"If we stop and think, we won't find a solution to the road back," said Slumber. "We had to get lost to get here and maybe there is some strange illogical way to get out of here too."

"Well, we'll have to figure them out both at the same time, otherwise one can't go without the other, can it now," said Eve, worried.

"Quite right, dear chicken, quite right," observed the Professor.

They all just sat there with chocolate cake in their mouths, staring at each other, wondering if they would have to go back to the farm without their camper or stay in the camper forever with no way back home.

Panic hit them. What if they never got out of there and had to spend another night?

"Well, no panic, everyone, we have to think with logical minds, and not all of us have that skill. So, the ones of you who are artistic are kindly requested to keep those thoughts in your heads, thank you, no offence, but each of us has a talent and now it's up to the logical species to take over," said Slumber.

"I don't quite agree with what you've just said," replied Eve. "But I get the sense of what your logical brain was trying to say. Now let me take my artistic brain back to bed so it can think in silence," she snapped as she went back upstairs to bed.

Everyone else sat there in a confused daze.

"If we can't get back, we'll leave the camper here and go back home by foot. We're not spending another night here. It just means it wasn't meant to be," said Kara and tranquilized everyone.

Kara, the Professor, Tobia, and Slumber went outside to see what could be done and how. The woods had a different look about them. The sun was shining from above and everything looked better, apart from the stink and the mold and the scary trees. But it didn't look as threatening as yesterday.

After a while, they were all outside. Some had gone to see if they could find the tiny road back, others were putting petrol in the camper, and still others were placing the planks of wood under the back wheels.

"Did you find anything?" asked Kara.

"Nope, no sign of a way out," said Gladys.

"The tank is full and ready," said Slumber.

"Professor, you go and put the engine on a second then we'll go on as planned," continued Slumber.

"Is everything ready for the ride, inside?" asked Tobia, worried for the whole situation in itself.

"Yes, Captain," said Elsa from the kitchen window.

"Good, then everybody come outside and go to the planks you were assigned to," Tobia remarked.

It was quite a sight to see. Tobia and Slumber were on one plank whilst Kara and the chickens on the other. As soon as the Professor hooted the horn, they started jumping to see if they could lift the wheels.

"One, two, three, JUMP!" shouted Tobia.

Nothing moved. They tried again and again but nothing happened.

"Ok, well, let's not give up now, lads, I'm quite sure we can make it. We just have to find the right idea to fit this plan," said the Professor.

"That's easier said than done now, isn't it?" Eve whispered to herself.

They tried putting two planks in the front of the camper and divided themselves into four groups of jumpers: the Professor and Elsa, Kara and Eve, Slumber on his own, and Gladys was obviously with Tobia.

They jumped all together, one, two, three, four times. Finally, the front wheels lifted slightly!

They jumped in happiness.

"Come on, lads, it's not over yet," encouraged the Professor. They put a rope around the tree in front of the camper and while Kara and the professor jumped with the various chickens, Slumber and Tobia pulled the rope, attached to the camper, around the tree.

As soon as the front wheels lifted, two chickens moved the wooden planks under each front wheel so that the wheel could sit on the plank and not on the mud.

They tried again. With a jump and a pull, and a jump and a pull, the wheels actually lifted from the mud and sat on the wood!

"Hurray," they all screamed.

"Now what we have to do is go far enough on the front planks to lift the back wheels," said Slumber.

They added another rope at the front and started pulling from both ends while the chickens kept jumping up and down on the planks.

"I've done enough exercise to last me till Christmas!" said breathless Gladys.

"Go on, ladies, you're doing great!" said Kara. She pulled the rope as hard as she could.

At a certain point they all fell on the ground while the chickens flew in the air and into the mud. The back wheels had popped out from the mud.

"Quickly, put the planks in front of the back wheels," yelled Slumber as he, Kara, and the Professor held the rope. Tobia helped the dirty chickens.

"One more time everybody," said Kara. "We can do it, we're a great team!"

They pulled and pulled and finally the camper was standing on four planks of wood in the middle of a muddy lake.

They were all exhausted and flopped on the ground!

"Great job, team! Now what we have to do is drive the camper as far as we can on the planks so as to bring it closer to dry land," instructed Slumber.

And so, they did. The camper slowly moved even if in a wobbly sort of way all the way to the tip of the front of all four planks.

"Damn," said Slumber. "We're off by half a plank!"

"I know," said Kara. "Let's get as much wood as possible and tie it together like a raft and see if that works."

The chickens and Tobia ran into the woods looking for long sticks of wood to tie together. They found only three. "We need more, for the other wheels."

"Wait a minute everyone." The Professor stopped. "If we carry the front wheels forward, the back wheels will drop off from the planks and fall back into the mud."

"Right you are, Professor," said Slumber.

"We have to put as much wood as possible to connect it to the planks so that the camper can keep rolling out."

At a certain point, they found a corner of the woods with branches which had fallen down during the storm. They tied them all together with the last pieces of rope and placed them under all the wheels.

"That should do it," Slumber remarked as he tied the last piece.

"Off we go. Tobia, it's your turn, you go behind the wheels and we'll pull."

"I'd love to, but my feet can't reach the pedals," he replied, slightly embarrassed.

"I'll help you," said Gladys. "You move the steering wheel and I'll sit on the pedals. I'm fat enough for them to go down." She giggled.

"Great," said Kara, anxious to finish. "Let's give it a try."

And so it was that even though it wobbled quite a lot, and they all held their breath, the camper slowly but surely made it across the planks of forest wood and plywood onto the dry land! They all cheered and hugged each other.

"Watch OUUUUUUT," yelled Slumber.

"Pull the hand break, Tobia, it's going backwards." There was a moment of general panic when, with a strong "screech," they managed to keep it still.

That was it, THE CAMPER WAS OUT!!

What a morning!

With the camper out of trouble, what they had to do next was find the road back home.

Elsa passed a glass of water and the last cookies to everyone.

"Bless you, sister," said Eve.

"You're welcome," replied Elsa, with a smile. It was nice to hear her sister say something like that for she was not typically one to give out compliments or loving affirmations.

They all jumped in. The Professor was at the wheel and Slumber right next to him as he started the engine. Kara and Tobia were outside to make sure it wouldn't fall back in the mud. As soon as the camper started moving, they jumped in.

"Where to?" said the Professor.

"I have no idea," said Slumber. "Let's try getting lost." They all laughed out loud and right that instant they all shut up. The trail was right in front of them. It seemed to be the same spot from where they had gotten all the broken branches from, but they were not sure.

The camper moved through all that strange silence everywhere. The sun started shining through the trees and the woods opened up as if to say goodbye. Nobody dared say anything. They all just watched the road ahead of them as the camper followed the road in the woods all the way to the main road.

They drove slowly and carefully and finally arrived at the front gate. Slumber jumped down to open it and let the camper in. They drove in. He closed the gate and jumped back in.

They drove all the way to the front of the house and when the Professor took the engine off, they all started screaming and shouting and hugging and crying. They had made it all the way home safe and sound and they now were the proud owners of an old white muddy camper and they couldn't be happier!

OOOOOOOOOOOOOOOOOOOOOOOOM. The camper dropped down lopsided and they all slid to the back of it in a bundle.

"I think a tire popped," said Slumber.

They all broke out in a laugh and carefully went out the front. I must say that was quite a sight to see, for every time someone tried to stand up, they would slide back down into the hump.... But between a push and a pull, they all managed to get out and put their feet on land.

Their land, their farm land.

"Well, everyone I am extremely proud of all of us," Kara said and started clapping her hands. There they stood clapping hands and watching the camper.

"Time for tea!!" shouted Elsa as she unlocked the front door. Tobia quickly put the fire on. He was good and fast with that sort of thing and they all plopped down in front of the fire with a warm cup of tea.

"What a day! What an adventure!" said Eve.

"Yes, it surely was and all thanks to you, Tobia old lad, all thanks to your curiosity!" remarked the Professor.

They laughed for the last time that afternoon because after that, they all fell asleep, as if someone had put them to sleep with a magic wand.

They slept and slept and the camper stood outside on its three wheels, looking at its new home.

CHAPTER 6

Back home

A couple of hours later, Grandma Violet softly walked into the room and woke Kara up. "It's seven o'clock, dear, you better get washed up and have an early supper. Tomorrow is school time again," she whispered.

All she could see was Kara laying on the sofa sleeping and all the animals fast asleep in front of the fire. Kara got up and showed her granny the camper. Violet was quite impressed with this house car even though she had no idea how it had gotten there. But she never asked too many questions, she accepted things the way they were. "Lovely," she said as she headed back to her house.

Kara woke her friends up and headed upstairs to take a warm shower and put some clean clothes on. They all did the same. It was quite strange to be separated again after two days of being close and living together. Everything seemed so big and the spaces so large but they soon got used to their independence again and it wasn't so bad after all.

The Professor took a warm shower, put the kettle on, refilled his pipe, and slipped into his warm pink slippers. "Oh, I did quite miss you," he said to himself, smiling as he sat on his chair and pulled a nice warm blanket over his legs. *I never thought I would make it back. There were moments when I really thought it was over, but thank goodness it is all finished now,* he thought. Everyone was home safe and he felt stronger somehow.

Slumber did the same, a warm shower was exactly what he needed. He pulled on his trousers and cozy sweater and cuddled up in his warm bed. He ran over everything that had happened since he had seen Tobia run off, and he never thought it would have been such a scary, crazy adventure, but he had managed to keep his cool and he was quite proud of that. Now that Kara had her dream come true, he felt good, accomplished, as if he had given her back what she had given him since the moment her father brought him to the farm. With that memory in mind, he fell asleep, back in his cozy bed.

As Tobia went back to his underground house, he thought of the last few days. He was quite happy about how everything had gone even though it had been the scariest time in his life. He realized he had been very brave; he probably was the first mole in his family to have been so courageous. As the warm water covered his body, he thought of how nice it had been to be part of a team and how nice it had felt to fall asleep all cuddled up with

Gladys. He didn't think chickens could be so warm. As he put some fresh clothes on, he couldn't get the thought out of his head that company was exactly what was missing in his life, even though he had it every day and he lived in a wonderful house with great friends. Still, something was missing in his life.

The hens wobbled upstairs. They were so tired, they had done so much more than they ever thought they could have, being chickens and all. They had done it together but the biggest sense of pride that they had was the fact that they had conquered their fears and that was a feeling that nothing else had ever given them before. As soon as they got up to their apartment, they spontaneously hugged each other. "We did it, girls," Elsa said and they hugged even tighter. They also took a warm shower and huddled on their sofas in the living room. "I suppose I should make something for dinner," said Elsa, "but I'm too tired."

"Oh, just relax, sis, you've done enough. I think everyone will make their own tonight. We all need rest," said Eve.

"I suppose you're right," she replied.

"Of course, I am," said Eve.

Elsa wobbled into bed. She didn't even get changed. The stress and emotion had been too much for her, but she had made it back. Her father would have been proud of her, she thought as she dozed off.

Eve changed and got into her nightgown. The memory of all that smashing and rain and noise would be with her forever. She shivered just thinking about it. As she crawled into bed, she thought about her sisters and how this had made them stronger than ever and closer, much closer. She couldn't have gone through this without them, the fear had been too much. "Now enough of that," she said to herself. "Just think that we're back and safe, and Kara has made her dream come true." With that thought in mind, she pulled the cover over her head and drifted off.

As Gladys looked outside, she could see Tobia's little house. *How nice it was to be together*, she thought. She felt sort of homesick as if something was missing in her life. Even though she had everything and everyone she could wish for, there was a sense of loneliness inside her.

Kara made herself a warm cup of soup and sipped it in bed with her warm pajamas on. Pebbles sat inside her crossed legs. Her school bag was all ready for tomorrow. She put the cup away, brushed her teeth, and burrowed under the comforter. She snuggled under all the way down with the blankets right over her head. Her back hurt as did her hands and feet, everything hurt, but it was a nice kind of hurt.

What a team we are, just like a real family, she thought as her eyes started to close.

"Goodnight, Pebbles, sleep well, see you tomorrow."

She fell asleep satisfied and proud, not only because she had made it home safe and taken care of everyone but because she had the most beautiful present destiny could have given her, a lovely camper, a house on wheels she could use to travel the world and see the things and places she had always wanted to see. That thought brought her back to her dreamland. A place she thought would remain just a land...but now was alive and waiting for her...With that image in mind, she fell into a deep sleep.

A soft breeze drifted over the farm. The camper in the front of the yard sat there lopsided; it too was now part of this family.

The next day Kara went off to school. Slumber opened the gate for her as usual and she hopped onto the school bus. Then he put his utensils belt on and went to the back of the farm next to the shed to see if he could find what he was looking for. He passed the Professor's house just as the Professor was coming out.

"Good morning."

"Good morning." The Professor followed him. They both knew what they were looking for.

"Wait for me," said Tobia.

The three of them walked together, not saying anything, a nice feeling of brotherhood warming them up.

In the meantime, the hens sat around the table. Elsa was sipping on her tea. Her wing hurt, so she didn't do much, while Gladys laid the table and put a pan of scrambled eggs and toast on it. Eve was in the back room looking for something, cackling away, complaining.

The lads came in. They must have found what they were looking for because they had smiles on their faces.

"Good morning, ladies," they said in unison. "Scrambled eggs, lovely breakfast idea," said Slumber.

"Are you quite all right, Elsa?" asked Tobia.

"She's hurt her wing. She needs to rest. We all do, actually," replied Gladys.

"Yes, I suppose a little rest will do everyone some good, but we have some work to do," said the Professor as they gobbled down their eggs and disappeared.

"So have I," said Eve as she moved the table cloth to make space for the sewing machine.

"What's that for?" asked Gladys.

"It's a sewing machine, need glasses?" replied Eve.

"No, I don't, thank you, and I can see that, smarty. I meant what do you need it for?"

"Well, why don't you ask THAT then?" Eve snapped. "I'm making new curtains for the camper. The ones it has now stink and they are quite horrid."

"Indeed," said the sisters.

Outside, the lads were busy changing the tire on the camper.

"Right, push it in, lads," said Slumber and so they did. The camper plopped back down looking quite new with that wheel.

"Everybody, move away!" said Tobia, a hose in his hands.

They all started washing and cleaning. Gladys brought the vacuum cleaner outside and vacuumed everything. They cleaned the toilet and the fridge and the kitchen and the floors. They removed all the blankets and comforters and put them in the wash.

"The sun is out, so they should be ready and crispy in a couple of hours," said Gladys.

Eve was working inside, putting in the new curtains, and the men opened the hood to work on the engine.

Everyone was busy, and by the time Kara's bus arrived, it was all done.

They all went to the gate to pick her up.

"Hello everyone, what a nice surprise to see you all here. Did something happen?" She didn't know whether to be happy or worried but she kept a smile on her face.

"Nothing to worry about, dear girl," said the Professor. "We have a surprise for you."

"Oh good" she said, relived.

They blindfolded her and led her down to the front of the house.

As soon as they got there, they took the blindfold off and moved into a circle around the camper.

"OH, MY GOODNESS!" she exclaimed. "How beautiful."

There it was, their camper, all clean and white, very white. The tires were so clean, they looked new. She ran to the side door.

"Just a second, me lady," said Slumber.

He opened the front door and pressed a button next to the driver's seat and down came a small set of stairs.

"Nooooo," said Kara. "This is pure magic," she said as she carefully climbed the steps to go inside.

When she walked in, she looked around. Everything was clean and smelt of lavender. The curtains were a beautiful yellow, as was the sofa and the tablecloth. They had also changed the curtain that separated the camper from the driver's area. They had put carpets on the floor and all the beds were made. Pebbles, walking under Kara's legs, stopped in awe.

Kara opened the bathroom and saw two carpets and new curtains. In the kitchen there were new kitchen cloths and a vase with freshly picked flowers. It was all so incredibly perfect and beautiful.

As she walked back down, tears of happiness rolled down her cheeks. They all hugged her and applauded together.

"I think this is the most beautiful thing I have EVER seen in my life. What an incredible job you all did!" said Kara.

Tobia closed the doors and stared at the camper with pride.

Gladys put her wing around him. "It is quite magical, isn't it?" she said in a loving voice

"Yes, quite, and so are you," he said as he put his arm around her.

They walked in to join the others who were sitting around the fireplace with a fresh cup of tea. Freshly baked muffins sat on a tray and Eve went round to give them each one. She put the tray down and sat next to Slumber on the sofa.

"What a lovely family we all are," she said, leaning her head on him.

"YES," said Kara. "We TRULY are."

"A family with a magic camper."

The fire sparkled away and the friends laughed, talking about the weekend and the adventure they had had. Pebbles sat outside staring at the camper. She didn't quite understand what it was, but it looked cozy to her, and that was enough for a cat. You see, friendship and family can often become the same thing. They are a feeling we have in our hearts, a feeling that keeps us warm and makes us feel good and special. That's what this family of friends was about. Each one of them had a special talent that made them who they were, they all accepted each other's differences, and even if they would quarrel once in a while, it was the respect and love they had for one another that brought them back together.

This "magically scary" adventure had brought them together in a way only it could have done. The struggles and the physical pain and the incredible amount of fear they had all felt blended in with their love and strength. Each one had brought something special to this adventure, each one had lived it in a special way and put it in their hearts as a memory. It was a strange memory, I must say, because it was filled with fear. A legend had come true and they had lived it. In all of this, they had to overcome their fears, and it would be a story they would pass on to future generations, the good and the bad. That's what life is about, memories we put in our hearts, hard or sad or happy or funny. Those memories are what make us who we are, and they are what we create every day to make *that day* special in its own way.

This camper had created *that* magic, in each of their hearts, and that was something they would take with them forever.

The wind whispered in the air and the sun slowly left its place as evening made its way in. The woods next door were still and scary as they had always been and that's the way they would stay for there was no reason for them to go back in there ever again. Actually, it was quite strange how they had managed to get out of there. The legend claimed that nobody had ever done that. Maybe it was the camper that managed to get them out. Maybe the trees had given up on them. Nobody would ever know, but that was ok too.

Kara's dream had come true and they were all stronger, they had conquered their fears, and that was one of the most difficult things do in life. It had made them all appreciate the simple life on the farm even more. Dreams do come true, even if sometimes to get there you have to go through the dark woods inside of you.

From the distance, whoever went by that farm could see a small light shining from the inside and a VERY white camper in the yard, just sitting there. There was a sense of peace and happiness that would make anyone smile.

Jessica loves to read, go to the movies, work in her garden, cook and travel in her family camper!

She was born to an Italian father and a Dutch mother in 1974. Jessica grew up overseas: 12 years in Africa, 4 years in Taiwan and 2 years in Australia. In 1993 she moved to Italy and graduated from the University of Torino with a bachelor's degree in Languages (English and Spanish Literature). She worked in the film\television\music industry as a makeup and sfx artist for 15 years. She also taught English in various levels of schooling. In 2006 she decided to move from the city life of Turin to the Tuscan countryside where she still lives with her husband, two daughters and dog.

After many years as a teacher Jessica decided to start writing, her long-life dream, and has now written her first children's book.

Her book *Kara and the Magic Camper* is about friendship, trust, honesty, lightness of spirit, team work and family. It is about a simple farm girl, Kara, who lives with her animals, her best friends. In this first book their adventure is quite bizarre, they want to bring home a camper which is stuck in the mud in the enchanted woods next to the farm.